KU-071-319

34134 00178949 1

Leabharlainn nan Eilean Siar

You can Save the Planet

A Bright Idea:
Conserving Energy

WESTERN ISLES
LIBRARIES

30575208J

J333.79

Tristan Boyer Binns

www.heinemann.co.uk/library

Visit our website to find out more information about Heinemann Library books.

To order:
- ☎ Phone 44 (0) 1865 888066
- 🖹 Send a fax to 44 (0) 1865 314091
- 💻 Visit the Heinemann Bookshop at www.heinemann.co.uk/library to browse our catalogue and order online.

First published in Great Britain by Heinemann Library, Halley Court, Jordan Hill, Oxford OX2 8EJ, part of Harcourt Education. Heinemann is a registered trademark of Harcourt Education Ltd.

© Harcourt Education Ltd 2005
The moral right of the proprietor has been asserted.

All rights reserved. No part of this publication may be reproduced, stored in a retrieval system, or transmitted in any form or by any means, electronic, mechanical, photocopying, recording, or otherwise, without either the prior written permission of the publishers or a licence permitting restricted copying in the United Kingdom issued by the Copyright Licensing Agency Ltd, 90 Tottenham Court Road, London W1T 4LP (www.cla.co.uk).

Editorial: Nancy Dickmann and Dave Harris
Design: Richard Parker and Q2A Solutions
Illustrations: Q2A and Jeff Edwards
Picture Research: Maria Joannou and Virginia Stroud-Lewis
Production: Camilla Smith

Originated by Dot Gradations Limited
Printed in China by WKT Company Limited

ISBN 0 431 04169 5
09 08 07 06 05
10 9 8 7 6 5 4 3 2 1

British Library Cataloguing in Publication Data
Binns, Tristan Boyer
A Bright Idea: Conserving Energy.
– (You Can Save the Planet)
333.7'9
A full catalogue record for this book is available from the British Library.

Acknowledgements
The publishers would like to thank the following for permission to reproduce photographs: Corbis p. **5**; Corbis/Derek Trask p. **9**; Corbis/Doug Wilson p. **4**; Corbis/Ferdaus Shamim p. **23**; Corbis/Hans Strand p. **17**; Corbis/James Leynse p. **14**; Corbis/Jim Cummins p. **12**; Corbis/Rob Lewine p. **15**; Corbis/Russell Munson p. **22**; Getty Images/Stone p. **27**; Panos Pictures p. **18**; Rex Features p. **26**; Robert Harding Picture Library p. **19**; Science Photo Library/Bernhard Edmaier p. **20**; Science Photo Library/Tony Craddock p. **21**; Science Photo Library/US Dept. Of Energy p. **25**; Science Photo Library/David R. Frazier p. **7**; Science Photo Library/John Keating p. **24**; Tudor Photography pp. **10**, **11**, **13**, **16**.

Cover photograph of a cyclist, reproduced with permission of Rex Features.

The publishers would like to thank Nick Lapthorn of the Field Studies Council for his assistance in the preparation of this book.

Every effort has been made to contact copyright holders of any material reproduced in this book. Any omissions will be rectified in subsequent printings if notice is given to the publishers.

The paper used to print this book comes from sustainable resources.

Disclaimer
All the internet addresses (URLs) given in this book were valid at the time of going to press. However, due to the dynamic nature of the Internet, some addresses may have changed, or sites may have ceased to exist since publication. While the author and publishers regret any inconvenience this may cause readers, no responsibility for any such changes can be accepted by either the author or the publishers.

Contents

Words appearing in the text in bold, **like this**, are explained in the Glossary.

What is energy?

Anything that does work uses energy. Work can be many things – a tomato plant growing, your body running, or your television showing you a video. Energy can be turned into different forms and stored.

Most of the energy used on the Earth comes from the Sun. Plants turn energy from sunlight into food. Plants then store energy themselves. Heat from the Sun makes the weather. This heat energy is stored in wind, rain, and waves. When we use energy, we take it out of its stored form.

When wood is burned, its energy is released as heat and light.

Plant energy

People and other animals use plants for their food. People also use products from plants, such as wood from trees, to burn for **fuel**. Huge numbers of plants and animals died millions of years ago. Their remains were covered by layers of soil and water. Their energy is now stored in oil, coal, and natural gas. We call these **fossil fuels**.

What does energy do for us?

People have always used energy to help make their lives easier. Long ago, simple machines such as levers used people's muscles for power. As machines became more complex they needed more power than people could give. Animals pulled ploughs to help grow food. Mills ground wheat into flour. They used wind or water for power.

Today we rely on very complex machines such as refrigerators and cars. Most modern machines are powered by electricity or engines that run on oil. Most of the power we use comes from fossil fuels. It is hard to imagine life without our machines and the energy that powers them.

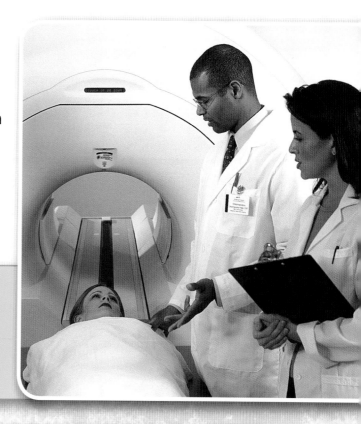

Some machines use energy to keep us healthy. This MRI machine can produce a picture of the inside of your body, but it needs electricity to run.

Taking Action

If we keep using so much energy, we are storing up problems for people in the future. You might think that the problem of saving, or conserving, energy is too big for you to do anything about. But if each of us makes a small effort, together we can make a big difference. Look out for Taking Action boxes like this one throughout this book. They will give you ideas for things you can do to conserve energy.

Getting energy home

Most of the energy we use at home and in school comes to us as electricity. It is made in an electricity factory called a **power plant**.

We also use other kinds of energy in our daily lives. Energy is used to make the things we buy, from clothes to packets of crisps. The lorries that transport these things to our shops use energy. We use all kinds of **fuels** directly. Petrol engines drive our cars, gas boilers heat our homes and water, and gas or electric cookers cook our food.

Science Behind It: Making electricity

Inside a power plant, fuel is used to drive a **turbine**. It usually heats water to make steam, which turns the turbine. The turbine looks like a pinwheel or propeller. As it spins, it makes an electricity **generator** work. The generator sends the electricity along wires to us.

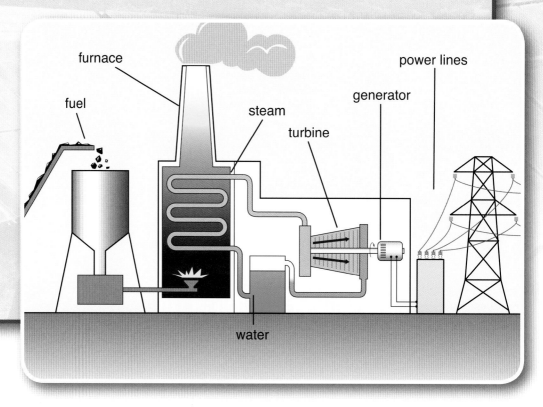

furnace

fuel

power lines

generator

steam

turbine

water

Why do we need to conserve energy?

You might think there is no need to conserve energy. Whenever you flip a switch, there is enough electricity to turn on the lights. But using too much energy has effects that are harder to see.

First, we are running out of **fossil fuels**. Fossil fuels are still forming in the Earth, but the process takes millions of years. Before the end of your life, we may run out of oil and gas. If we can use fewer fossil fuels now, the supply we have now will last longer.

Also, when we burn fossil fuels for energy they give off gases. Some of these gases **pollute** our air and water. This can make the air unsafe to breathe and the water unsafe to drink. One of the main gases produced is **carbon dioxide**. Carbon dioxide is not bad by itself. Plants need it to make their food. The problem is that we are making too much of it.

In cities where a great deal of fossil fuels are burned, the air looks hazy because of pollution.

Climate change happens naturally over long periods of time. We are making it happen much faster by making gases such as carbon dioxide, and the planet is heating up. We need to stop climate change before the Earth changes so much that it is hard for us to live on it.

Science Behind It: The greenhouse effect

When carbon dioxide sits in the air it makes an invisible shield, like a pane of glass in a greenhouse. The Sun's heat gets in through the shield, but then it gets trapped. The extra heat is making our planet warm up. This is called the greenhouse effect.

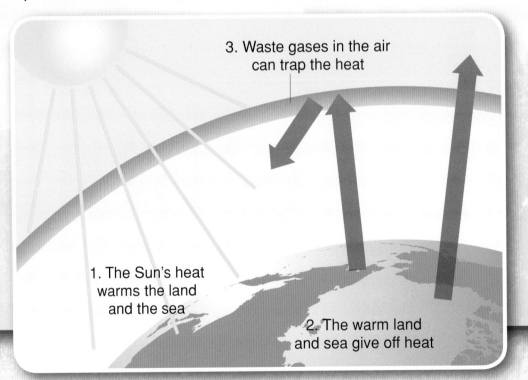

3. Waste gases in the air can trap the heat

1. The Sun's heat warms the land and the sea

2. The warm land and sea give off heat

Making changes

We can help to prevent these problems. One way is to find other sources of energy. Some types, such as wind and solar power, are **renewable**. They are made by the Sun and cannot be used up. Another way is to use energy more **efficiently** so we waste less.

How is energy wasted?

At home and at school, energy is used and wasted in similar ways. Scientists think that we waste about half of the energy we use.

Energy keeping us warm

At home, we use the most energy for heating. All of these waste energy:

- badly **insulated** walls
- cracks in floorboards and around doors and windows
- draughty windows
- lofts without insulation
- uninsulated hot water pipes and tanks
- water heated hotter than we need
- room heat turned up high when an extra jumper would do
- windows or doors left open when the heating or air conditioning is on
- curtains left open on a cold night.

Transport wastes

Taking the car more than you need to wastes energy. Could you combine errands and visits to save journeys? Can you share a ride? A car wastes more energy than cycling, walking, or taking the bus or train.

Travelling with only one person in a car wastes a lot of energy. Sharing rides or going by **public transport** saves energy, and puts less **carbon dioxide** into the air.

Wasting electricity

Whenever you waste electricity, you waste energy. If you do any of these things, you will waste electricity:

- leaving lights on when you leave a room
- leaving machines on or in standby mode. Many photocopiers, computers, and televisions are left on overnight.
- leaving the fridge door open.

Machines such as cars, boilers, and lawnmowers work best when they are properly serviced. Some have filters to clean and fluids to top up. If they are not working at their best, they use energy less **efficiently**.

Science Behind It: Losing power

Every way of making power costs energy. For example, batteries take fifty times as much energy to make as they can give out. When coal is burned in a **power plant** only some of its energy is made into electricity. Most of the rest is lost as heat. More energy is lost as the electricity travels along wires to buildings.

These machines can use almost as much energy in standby mode as they do when turned on completely.

How can we conserve energy?

Every day, you make hundreds of choices. Some will save energy and some will use it. You have the power to make choices that will help change the Earth for the better.

Reduce, reuse, recycle

Energy is used every time something new is made. Here is a great way to start conserving energy: reduce what you use, reuse what you can, and **recycle** as much of your waste as possible. For example, reduce the number of plastic carrier bags you use by bringing old ones with you to the shops to reuse. When they cannot be used any more, most supermarkets will take them back to recycle.

Taking Action: Using less

Here are some other ways to reduce and reuse around your home:

- reuse envelopes with sticky labels
- draw or print on both sides of paper
- send e-cards instead of paper ones
- use libraries and rental shops instead of buying new books, videos, or DVDs
- wash out and reuse sandwich bags and water bottles
- use cloths and sponges instead of paper kitchen roll
- instead of throwing old things out, give them to charity shops.

Recycled plastic can be used to make many things, such as these fleece jackets and refuse bags.

Using less energy

Around the house and at school, you can make energy-saving choices. Simply turning off things when you finish using them will help a lot. When a television or computer is in standby mode it still uses energy, so switch it off completely. Turn lights off when you leave a room. Dry your clothes and wet hair in the open air when you can. Only run the dishwasher or washing machine when they are full.

It takes energy to heat water. It also takes energy to make water clean and get it to our houses to use. You can choose to save water and save energy too. Have a shower instead of a bath – this will save both water and energy! Don't leave the tap running while you do the washing up or clean your teeth.

Taking Action: Free time

One more way to conserve energy is to think about what you do for fun. Shopping and playing computer games use electricity. What do you do that does not use electricity? Playing football, chatting with your friends, training with the swim team – what else? These all use a type of **renewable** energy – yours!

Playing ball games uses a lot of energy, but you do not have to burn any **fossil fuels** to do it!

12

Making Choices

Some of the best ways to conserve energy are to choose more **efficient** ways to do things. You need light bulbs to light the rooms in your house. But changing normal light bulbs to special low-energy ones saves a huge amount of energy.

If every household in the UK changed just three bulbs to low energy bulbs, it would save enough energy in a year to pay for the entire country's street lighting!

Some family choices can make big savings. You could research these with your parents. When your family needs new appliances, look at the energy labels to choose the most efficient ones. When your parents are choosing a car, encourage them to get one that will use the least amount of **fuel**.

Using the Internet or catalogues to shop saves energy. Food, clothes, books, and other items are stored in big warehouses. They use less energy to run than shops do. One van can deliver to many households, instead of many families driving their cars to the shops.

Saving energy on food

You need to eat, but you can choose food grown or made near your home by shopping at farmers' markets. Local food is not transported far, so it takes less energy to make. The packaging your food comes in takes energy too. Think about all the snack wrappers and drinks cartons you throw away. Could you save energy and waste by reusing bags and bottles to make home-packaged snacks and drinks?

All this waste cost energy to produce. It took energy to bring it to this landfill site too.

The way to school

In developed countries like the UK, the USA and Australia, driving children to school is a huge energy drain. Walking or cycling may be a great way to save energy and help keep you fit. School buses use a lot of fuel, which is made from oil. They can be changed so that they run on cleaner fuel and use less energy.

Taking Action: Transport savings

You can help save energy getting to school. You could start a group working with other students, parents, and teachers. Take **surveys** of how people get to school. Look into other ways you could get to school using less fuel. Check out government schemes that offer money and help. Come up with a plan and present it to your school governors.

Case Study: Saving energy at school

Students can look at how their school uses energy and find ways to conserve it. Sulzberger Middle School in Philadelphia, USA, joined the Green Schools programme. It won an Earth Apple award for how well it saved energy. Students and teachers worked together. They made posters saying 'Save Energy'. They made a video about saving energy. They also formed an Energy Patrol. The Energy Patrol looked for classrooms that wasted energy by leaving windows open, lights on, and blinds up. Energy wasters were fined 10 cents, about 6 pence.

To save energy, you should switch off the electric lights in your classroom when there is enough light coming through a window.

Success!

After one school year, no one was fined anymore. Sulzberger Middle School saved 194,230 kilowatt hours of electricity. This was almost half of what they had used the year before! Savings this high mean good things for the Earth. Such savings also mean the school has more money to spend on books and other materials.

CASE STUDY

What is the problem with fossil fuels?

There are three kinds of **fossil fuels**: coal, oil, and natural gas. Of these, we have the most coal left. But coal is not used as much as it once was, since it is more **polluting** and less **efficient** to burn. We have about 70 years' worth of natural gas left. This is cleaner to burn and can be burned in homes to power their heating systems. This makes it more efficient.

We only have about 40 years' worth of oil left, because we use it so quickly. Oil is made into many things. Some examples are petrol and diesel to run engines, jet **fuel** for aeroplanes, and oil for **power plants**.

Taking Action: Oil in the home

Oil can be made into chemicals that help to make all of these things.

Make a list. How many of these things are in your life? These are all made from oil:
- plastic bags
- tyres
- plastic toys
- rubber wellies
- food wrappers
- nylon and polyester clothes.

What other materials could you use now to replace these plastics and rubbers? How could you use less in the first place?

What other kinds of fuel are there?

Fossil fuels power most of the world. But other fuels are used more and more. Different places can use different kinds of fuel.

In some places, the hot liquid rock inside the Earth comes near the surface. The hot rock heats water in the ground above it. The water comes out as hot springs or steam. It can be turned into **renewable geothermal** energy. Geothermal energy is not perfect. Some pollution comes out of the ground with the steam. Some **carbon dioxide** is given off. But the amounts are very low compared to burning fossil fuels.

Science Behind It: Geothermal power

In a **power plant**, fuel is usually burned to make steam that then turns a **turbine**. A geothermal power plant simply skips the burning stage. The steam comes directly from the ground and then turns the turbines. Electricity is made and sent along wires in the normal way. Geothermal power can also make hot water and steam heat to be sent straight to homes.

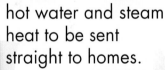

In Iceland, geothermal energy is used for most of the electricty and heating. These people are bathing in the hot water near the power station!

What is bioenergy?

Everything that comes from plants and animals is called **biomass**. Biomass can be used to make **bioenergy**. Bioenergy makes no more carbon dioxide than the biomass would give off if it **decayed** naturally. Because biomass comes from growing things, it is renewable.

The most popular kind of biomass is wood. Many people burn wood in their homes for cooking and heating. Huge **power plants** also burn wood and other plants to make electricity. Biomass can also be made into liquid **biofuels**. Some biofuel is made from the vegetable oil used to fry chips! Some biofuel is made from plants left over after being used for their main purpose, such as sugar cane. Biofuels can be added to or used instead of petrol and diesel.

This is a biogas generator being used to make power for a home in Nepal.

When biomass is heated in a closed space, it gives off a gas. This gas can be used for energy. Farming families in poor countries can use small systems to change their animals' dung into this **biogas** to cook and heat with. A bigger system can collect the biogas given off by rubbish dumped at a landfill site. The biogas is burned in power plants to make electricity.

Nuclear power

A nuclear power plant has a **reactor** where **uranium** fuel is used to heat water. The hot water makes steam, just as it does in fossil fuel power stations. The steam turns a turbine to make electricity.

Nuclear power is not renewable, because the uranium has to be dug from the ground. We will eventually run out of uranium. Nuclear power makes no carbon dioxide, so it does not add to **climate change**. But it does make very dangerous waste. Some gets into the air and water near power plants. It can make people and animals very ill. Uranium waste can stay dangerous for more than 10,000 years. No one is sure what to do with it until then.

Science Behind It: Splitting atoms

A nuclear reactor makes heat by splitting **atoms** of uranium into even smaller parts. When they split, they give off energy. This reaction is controlled very carefully. If it got out of control, dangerous materials could be let out. New reactors are planned that will make it easier to control.

This is a nuclear power station by the sea.

Water power

Water can be used to make electricity. Water power is renewable. **Hydroelectric** power plants use dams across rivers to trap water. Tidal power plants trap water behind gates in rivers as the tide comes in. When power is needed, the trapped water is let out. It flows over turbines. The turbines make generators run, and electricity is made.

Waves can also make power. As they rise and fall, they move air inside a tube. The moving air turns a turbine. But waves have so much power they break the machines easily.

Many people think that the costs from huge dam projects are higher than the benefits of clean electricity.

When dams and tidal gates are built, they flood land. Big projects mean whole towns and farms are lost. The places where plants and animals live are gone forever. Small projects can still make enough power for a town without hurting the land around it.

Solar power

Wherever it is sunny a lot of the time, solar energy can be used. The Sun's energy is renewable. It can be used in a number of ways. It can be focused by mirrors on to one spot. In a solar cooker, the focused energy can cook a family's meal. In a solar power plant, the energy is used to make steam. The steam spins the turbines and makes electricity.

This is a huge sunlight reflector in France.

In many homes, solar energy is used to heat water. Pipes are built into panels on the roof. Cold water goes in and is heated by the Sun to come out hot. The water goes straight into the hot water tank.

Science Behind It: Solar panels

Solar panels contain cells that are made from a material called **silicon**. The panels take sunlight and turn it directly into electricity. They are expensive to make. It takes a lot of them to make enough power for the needs of a whole house. But they can be used anywhere, and they do not break down. Thousands of panels linked together can run solar power plants.

Hi-tech windmills

Wherever it is windy a lot of the time, windmills can be used to collect energy. Wind energy is renewable. Most of today's windmills have blades that look like aeroplane propellers. They spin and turn gears inside the windmill. The gears turn an electricity **generator**. One windmill can power a single home. Grouped together in a wind farm they can make a huge amount of power.

This wind farm uses a lot of land but makes a lot of electricity.

Sight and sound

Windmills are huge. The blades are high up, where the wind is strongest, so they are hard to hide. Many people think wind farms are ugly. Windmills make no air **pollution**, but they do make noise pollution. Sometimes wind farms can be built in shallow water off a coastline. They cost more to build there, but they make more power and are farther away from where people live.

Batteries and fuel cells

The problem with solar and wind energy is that they depend on weather or **climate** conditions, so they cannot be used everywhere. Batteries and **fuel cells** store power so they can be used when it is not sunny or windy.

Batteries are made from chemicals that give off power when they react with each other. Small batteries run small things such as toys, but big ones can power a house. Fuel cells are much more **efficient** than batteries at making power. They can run spacecraft and cars. Most are recharged with hydrogen.

Science Behind It: How a fuel cell works

Water is made up of hydrogen and oxygen. A fuel cell is charged with hydrogen. When power is needed, it pulls oxygen from the air. The oxygen mixes with the hydrogen to make water. When the water is made, energy is given off for the fuel cell to use as electricity. The water and power are the only things the fuel cell makes. It does not make any pollution.

This is a car with a fuel cell engine, which makes no pollution.

Case Study: Eco Schools

Schools in Europe can join the Eco Schools programme. The programme has many ideas for how to make schools more Earth-friendly. One focus is on energy. Wilnecote Junior School is an Eco School in the UK that runs on electricity. The school wanted to save money and use less electricity.

This building has lots of solar panels to make electricity. Could you use a solar panel at home or school?

Solar walkway

Students and teachers came up with a plan to build a walkway with a solar panel on the top. The solar panel makes enough power to light classrooms and run computers. To tell people about their success, the school has a display by the office. The display says how much power is being made at any time, and how much has been made since the panel was put in. Wilnecote still has to buy some electricity but much less than before.

Paying for the change

Wilnecote did not have to pay for the whole cost of the project by itself. The government and some businesses paid for more than half of the solar panel and walkway. There are **grants** like this for schools and people who want to be more energy-**efficient**.

Biomass central heating

In Slovenia, one Eco School has made a big change. Students and teachers at the Sv. Trojica primary school looked at how their school used energy. They decided to change the way the central heating system was powered. After looking at their **renewable** energy choices, they chose to use a **biomass** boiler. Their boiler burns wood to heat the school.

Opening Ceremony

When the new boiler was ready to run, Sv. Trojica had an opening ceremony. They invited students and important people from their town. The president of the Slovenian biomass group helped out. Sv. Trojica is proud to be the only school in Slovenia using wood biomass for its central heating system.

This man is putting wood chips into a machine to make the fuel for a biomass boiler.

What will happen next?

As we run out of **fossil fuels** and create more **pollution**, we will have to use more and more **renewable** energy. Even though we already have some good sources of renewable energy, new sources are being researched every day.

Cool water makes cool air

Some experts try thinking about what we need instead of how we get it. In Ithaca, New York, there is a big lake full of cool water. In the heat of the summer, the cool water could be pumped to shore. It could make cool air for air conditioning. The water would cool hot air in a heat exchanger. The warmed water would run back into the lake but would not be hot enough to harm wildlife. This is also being tried in other cities by big lakes in Sweden, Canada, and Hawaii.

The American Solar Challenge shows how well renewable energy can work. This 3700 kilometre (2300 mile) car race is only open to cars that run on solar power.

Fuel cells

New kinds of **fuel cells** look very promising. One type is made with natural gas. It does not actually burn the gas. Instead it uses a chemical reaction to make the power. This fuel cell is very quiet, gives off little pollution, and seems very **efficient**. Even though it still uses a fossil fuel, it uses the **fuel** in a better way.

There is a kind of algae that gives off hydrogen in water. If enough hydrogen could be collected from the algae, it could make the fuel for hydrogen fuel cells. Other types of plants may help make more **bioenergy**. A special kind of seaweed grows up to a metre a day. If it was farmed and used to make **biogas**, it could produce a lot of power.

Taking Action: Energy club

Using what you have learned so far, think about how you could use renewable energy in your home or school. How can you save energy as well? Start an energy club and research what would work for you. Don't forget to investigate the **grants** that are available to help pay for changes.

Some newer kitchen appliances contain computers that control how they work. This means they work more efficiently and use less energy.

fact file

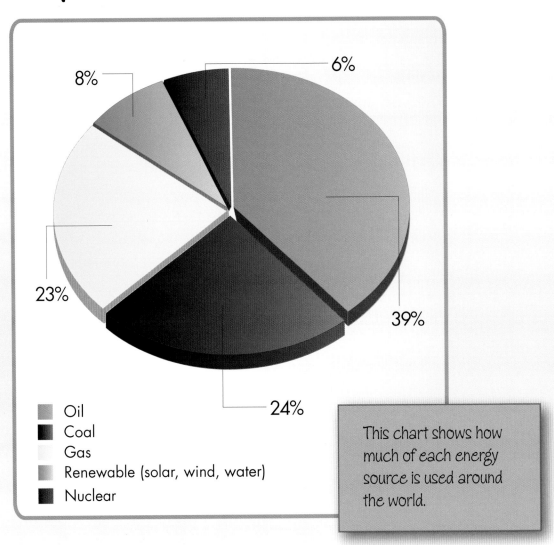

8%   6%

23%

39%

24%

Oil
Coal
Gas
Renewable (solar, wind, water)
Nuclear

This chart shows how much of each energy source is used around the world.

- In the UK, 80% of the energy which is used for transport is used by private cars.
- In rural China, two-thirds of homes use **biogas**.
- In the United States, almost 4% of all energy used is **bioenergy**.
- In the UK, almost 3% of energy comes from **renewable** sources.

Find out more

Books to read

Alternative Energy Sources, Sally Morgan (Heinemann Library, 2002)

Earth's Precious Resources: Fossil Fuels, Ian Graham (Heinemann Library, 2004)

Green Files: Future Power, Steve Parker (Heinemann Library, 2004)

New Energy Sources, Nigel Hawkes (Franklin Watts, 2000)

Websites

There are many useful websites to help you learn more and make plans for taking action of your own.

Eco-Schools – a website about Eco Schools in the UK:
www.eco-schools.org.uk

Sustrans – information about sustainable transport:
www.sustrans.org.uk

The Australian Greenhouse Office – a site about alternative energy:
www.greenhouse.gov.au

Green Schools – learn about making schools more energy-efficient:
www.ase.org/greenschools

The Centre for Alternative Technology – Europe's leading eco-centre :
www.cat.org.uk

Glossary

atom smallest part of a chemical, such as an atom of oxygen

bioenergy energy made from biomass

biofuel fuel made from biomass, such as vegetable oil

biogas gas made from biomass, such as methane gas

biomass everything that comes from plants and animals, including manure

carbon dioxide gas made from carbon and oxygen that adds to climate change. It is also used by plants to make their food.

climate what the temperature, wind, humidity, rainfall, and other weather is like in an area

climate change as we add to the layer of gases that surround Earth, different climates around the world may get warmer or colder, wetter or dryer. No one is sure how much change will happen.

decay what happens after things die when they break down and rot

efficient using a resource, such as energy or water, so that as little as possible is wasted

fossil fuel fuel that is formed from the remains of plants and animals that died millions of years ago. Fossil fuels include coal, gas, and oil.

fuel something that can be burned to create heat or power

fuel cell machine that makes power from hydrogen

generator machine that makes energy

geothermal describes energy that comes from the heat deep within the Earth

grant money given to help buy or change something, such as changing the kind of fuel an engine uses to a less polluting one

hydroelectric electricity made from water as it flows over turbines

insulate keep heat, sound, or electricity from escaping and being wasted

pollution something that makes air, water, or other parts of the Earth's environment dirty

power plant place where electricity is made

public transport buses, trains, trams, and any kind of transport that can be used by many people

reactor place in a nuclear power plant where uranium is used to make heat and then power

recycle collect things made from a material that can be broken down and remade into new things, such as newspapers, plastic or glass bottles

renewable something that does not run out when we use it, such as solar energy

silicon material that helps change sunlight into electricity in solar panels

survey list of questions and answers that helps you find out information

turbine machine driven by water or steam that turns or spins

uranium material that comes from Earth that can be used to make nuclear power

Index

Titles in the *You Can Save The Planet* series include:

Hardback   0 431 04168 7

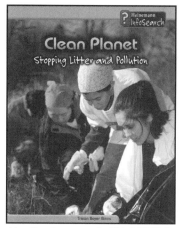

Hardback   0 431 04171 7

Hardback   0 431 04169 5

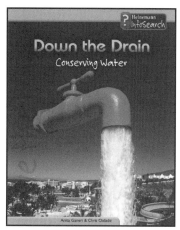

Hardback   0 431 04170 9

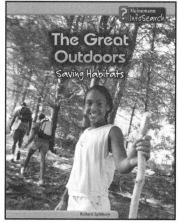

Hardback   0 431 04172 5

Find out about other titles from Heinemann Library on our website www.heinemann.co.uk/library